Class Clowns

by Meish Goldish
illustrated by Pat Paris

Scott Foresman

Editorial Offices: Glenview, Illinois • New York, New York
Sales Offices: Reading, Massachusetts • Duluth, Georgia
Glenview, Illinois • Carrollton, Texas • Menlo Park, California

Hello! Welcome to the "Big Top." That's what we here call the circus. I work here as a clown. Let me introduce myself. I'm the one with the pie in my face!

It is lots of fun being a clown. But it's not easy to become one. I had to be patient. First, I had to take classes at a special school. I'm not kidding! I was trained to be a clown.

Getting into clown school wasn't easy. Lots of people wanted to go there. There wasn't room for all of us. We had to audition, or try out. We had to act silly and do funny tricks. In the end, they chose only a few of us.

In most schools, you can't clown
around. But in this school, they want
us to clown around! Even the teachers
are clowns. Most of them have worked
in the circus.

Clown school is really fun!

In one class, we learned to walk on sticks called stilts. At first, it was hard. My teacher showed me how to do it without falling over. After that, I felt much safer!

I learned to ride a unicycle too.
That's a bike with just one wheel. It's
really neat! My teacher showed me
how to balance on it. Now I can zip
around the ring in any direction. I'm
starting to get my act together!

Have you ever walked on a high
wire? We learned how—one step at a
time! I admit it was scary at first. I
wore a harness to be safe. They also
put a net under us in case we fell.
And we did! But we were patient. Now
I can walk the wire without a net
or harness.

I can keep five rings in the air at once. It took me a long time to learn this trick. I started with just two rings. Then I used three, then four, and then five. The secret is to keep your eyes on the right spot at all times.

A clown must be in good shape to run around the circus ring. In school, we worked out together each day. We ran around in every direction. We fell down and rolled over. Then we got right back up on our feet.

Run! Fall! Roll! Stand! Clowning sure has its ups and downs!

Clowns love water! In school, we learned how to shoot big bottles of water at each other. We even learned how to spit water a long way! It's not as easy as you may think. (Here's a hint: Wear a raincoat!)

Clowns always have to look their best! Our teachers guide us to use many kinds of make-up. As you can see, I like bright colors. And I love my red nose and my wig.

How do you like my funny coat?
How about my baggy pants and big
shoes? You would never dress this
way in your school. But in clown
school, they guide us toward a
different dress code: Look silly!

School lasted eight weeks. On the last day of class, we had a big party. Everyone did tricks.

How do you like my special trick?
Everyone in class loved it!

These days, I work as a circus
clown. I travel to many interesting
places. I meet lots of different people,
both big and little.

I know just how to make them
smile—thanks to clown school!